W9-API-439

FREEDOM'S
PROMISE

THE
NEGRO
LEAGUES

BY DUCHESS HARRIS, JD, PHD

WITH ALEX KIES

Core Library

An Imprint of Abdo Publishing
abdobooks.com

Cover image: Leroy "Satchel" Paige was a skilled
pitcher in the Negro Leagues.

abdobooks.com

Published by Abdo Publishing, a division of ABDO, PO Box 398166, Minneapolis, Minnesota 55439. Copyright © 2020 by Abdo Consulting Group, Inc. International copyrights reserved in all countries. No part of this book may be reproduced in any form without written permission from the publisher. Core Library™ is a trademark and logo of Abdo Publishing.

Printed in the United States of America, North Mankato, Minnesota
092019
012020

THIS BOOK CONTAINS RECYCLED MATERIALS

Cover Photo: Matty Zimmerman/AP Images
Interior Photos: Matty Zimmerman/AP Images, 1, 28–29; AP Images, 5; Harry Harris/AP Images, 6–7, 33, 43; Picture History/Newscom, 9; Bettmann/Getty Images, 14–15, 20–21; Diamond Images/Getty Images, 17; Marion Post Wolcott/Farm Security Administration/Glasshouse Images/Newscom, 23; Red Line Editorial, 25, 41; TSN/Icon SMI/Newscom, 31; Minnesota Historical Society/Corbis Historical/Getty Images, 36–37; San Diego Union-Tribune/Zuma Press/Newscom, 38

Editor: Maddie Spalding
Series Designer: Ryan Gale

Library of Congress Control Number: 2019942096

Publisher's Cataloging-in-Publication Data

Names: Harris, Duchess, author | Kies, Alex, author.
Title: The negro leagues / by Duchess Harris and Alex Kies
Description: Minneapolis, Minnesota : Abdo Publishing, 2020 | Series: Freedom's promise | Includes online resources and index.
Identifiers: ISBN 9781532190872 (lib. bdg.) | ISBN 9781532176722 (ebook)
Subjects: LCSH: Negro leagues--United States--Juvenile literature. | African American baseball players--Juvenile literature. | Baseball--United States--History--20th century--Juvenile literature. | Discrimination in sports--United States--History--Juvenile literature. | Minorities in sports--Juvenile literature.
Classification: DDC 796.3576408--dc23

CONTENTS

A LETTER FROM DUCHESS

I threw out the ceremonial first pitch prior to the Minnesota Twins' July 20, 2019, game at Target Field against the Oakland A's. This was a tremendous honor for several reasons, and I am aware that this could not have happened in my parents' or grandparents' generations.

Throughout the late 1800s and early 1900s, professional baseball was segregated in the United States. Many major and minor leagues would not accept Black ballplayers. This exclusion forced Black ballplayers to form their own leagues: the Negro Leagues. This book tells the story of the pride that many people had in the Negro Leagues. It also explores how people of African descent desegregated baseball.

Today, we consider baseball to be one of America's greatest pastimes. I challenge you to think about who has historically been included—and who has been excluded—from this sport. Please join me on a journey to learn about the Negro Leagues and their legacy.

Duchess Harris

Leroy "Satchel" Paige, *right*, a former Negro League pitcher, sits with fellow pitcher Bob Feller, *left*, in the dugout before a game.

CHAPTER ONE

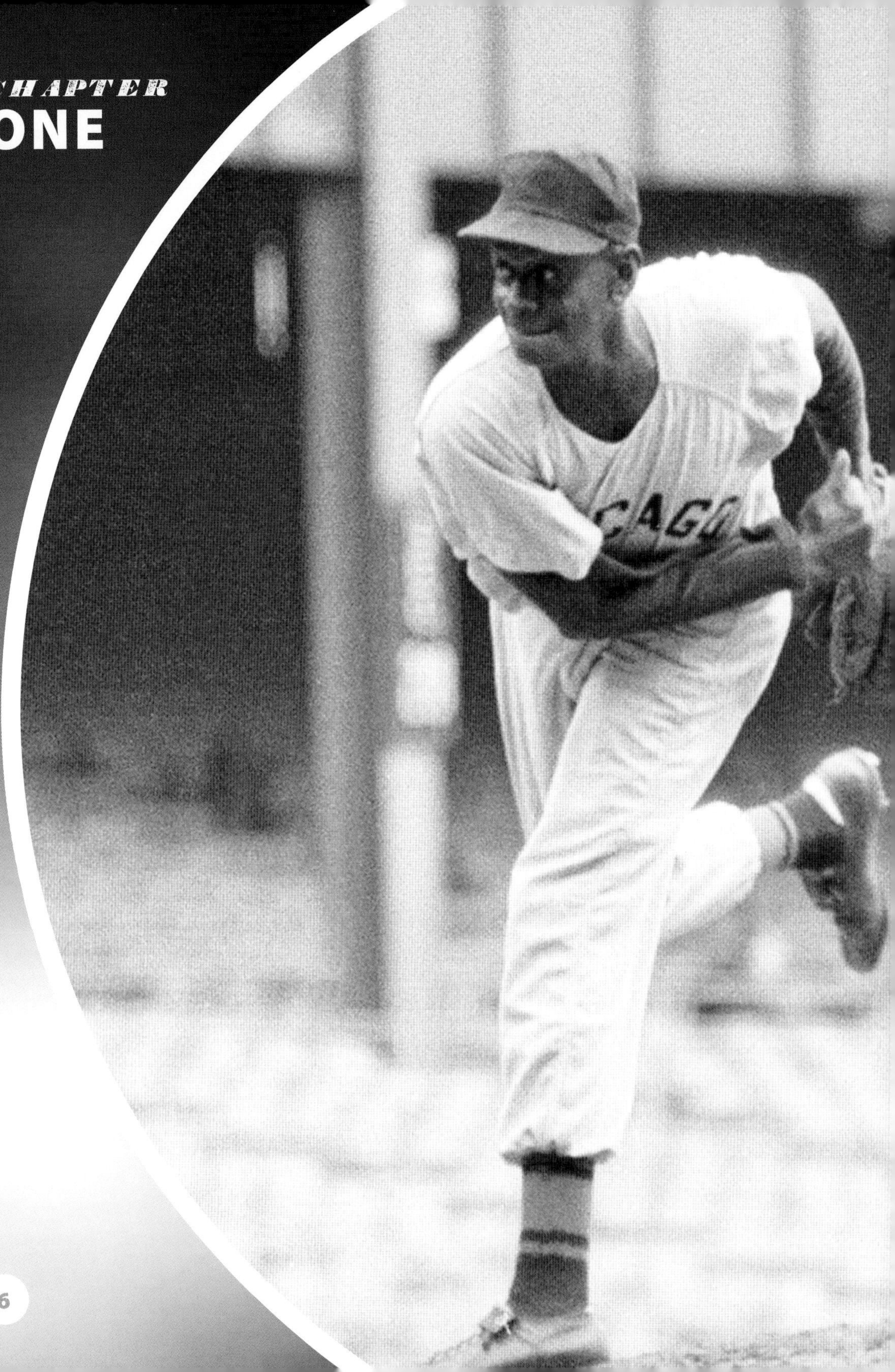

THE COLOR BARRIER

On January 26, 1936, two baseball legends faced each other for the first time. Joe DiMaggio and Leroy "Satchel" Paige arrived with their teams at Oaks Ball Park in Emeryville, California. DiMaggio was a white minor league baseball player. Paige was an African American baseball player. He was known as the best pitcher in the Negro Leagues, an association of Black baseball leagues.

Approximately 4,000 fans arrived to watch the exhibition game. Many came to see Paige. He pitched terrifically, only allowing one run through nine innings. He threw a fastball that

Satchel Paige pitched 2,500 games throughout his baseball career, which spanned nearly 30 years.

many players could not hit. He had many different pitching styles. One of his favorites was the hesitation pitch. He paused in the middle of his delivery. This threw off the batters' timing.

DiMaggio came up to the plate in the tenth inning. He hit a single up the middle that drove in the winning run. DiMaggio later called Paige the greatest pitcher he'd ever faced.

Newspapers across the country praised Paige. Many baseball officials were impressed with him too. But Major League Baseball (MLB) teams would not hire him because of his skin color. At the time, African Americans were banned from the major leagues.

SEGREGATION

Segregation in baseball was part of a larger problem in the United States at the time. Segregation laws separated Black and white people. These laws were called Jim Crow laws. Black people had to use separate

Paige, *standing*, *left*, was on the all-Black professional baseball team the Pittsburgh Crawfords from 1931 to 1937.

services and facilities, such as bathrooms. Professional sports were segregated too.

Baseball's early history can be traced back to the early and mid-1800s. In 1867 the National Association of Base Ball Players created the sport's first color barrier. The association was an organization of more than 300 baseball clubs. It did not allow clubs with Black players to join.

In 1876 the National League of Professional Baseball Clubs was formed. This professional baseball league is still active today. Those who formed the National League came up with an agreement. They would not allow Black players into the league.

BLACK BALLPLAYERS

Not all leagues enforced a color barrier. Two African Americans played in the American Association—a rival to the National League—in 1884. They were Moses Fleetwood Walker and his brother, Welday Walker. Moses had made his major league debut in 1884 for the Toledo Blue Stockings. He was the first professional Black ballplayer.

By 1887 there were 13 Black ballplayers on 12 minor league teams. Many played in the International League. This was a minor league just below the level of the major leagues.

On July 14, 1887, two baseball teams prepared to play an exhibition game in Newark, New Jersey. The Chicago White Stockings played in the National League, which was segregated. The Little Giants played in the

International League, which was not. George Stovey played for the Little Giants. He was an African American pitcher. Adrian "Cap" Anson was the White Stockings' manager. When he saw who was pitching for the Little Giants that day, he said he would not let his team play.

Anson's threat worked. Stovey did not play that day. The International League took action to avoid similar confrontations in the future. It forbade

THE CUBAN GIANTS

In 1885 waiter Frank Thompson formed a baseball team with his coworkers at the Argyle Hotel in New York City. They were all African American. They played against visiting teams in a field behind the hotel. Businessman Walter Cook helped Thompson's team go professional in 1886. Cook worried that fans would not pay to see an all-Black team. So he named the team the Cuban Giants. He thought white audiences would be less prejudiced against Cubans than against African Americans. But many people figured out that the players were African American. This angered some fans and journalists. Some newspapers insulted the Giants.

its teams from signing Black players.

After the International League banned the signing of Black players, other leagues followed suit. So Black ballplayers formed their own teams. They would later form their own leagues. Negro League players faced many obstacles both on and off the field. But they persevered. Their legacy is an important part of baseball's history.

STRAIGHT TO THE
SOURCE

John "Bud" Fowler was a Black minor league baseball player in the late 1800s. Like many Black players, Fowler struggled after leagues became segregated. In an 1895 interview with *Sporting Life* magazine, he said:

> *It was hard picking for a colored player this year. I didn't pick up a living; I just existed. I was down in the lower Illinois country and in Missouri, cross-roading with teams in the little towns. . . . My skin is against me. If I had not been quite so black, I might have caught on as a Spaniard or something of that kind. The race prejudice is so strong that my black skin barred me.*

Source: Robert Peterson. *Only the Ball Was White: A History of Legendary Black Players and All-Black Professional Teams.* Englewood Cliffs, NJ: Prentice-Hall, 1970. Print. 40.

Point of View
Take a close look at this passage. What was Fowler's situation like at this time? How did racial discrimination affect him?

CHAPTER TWO

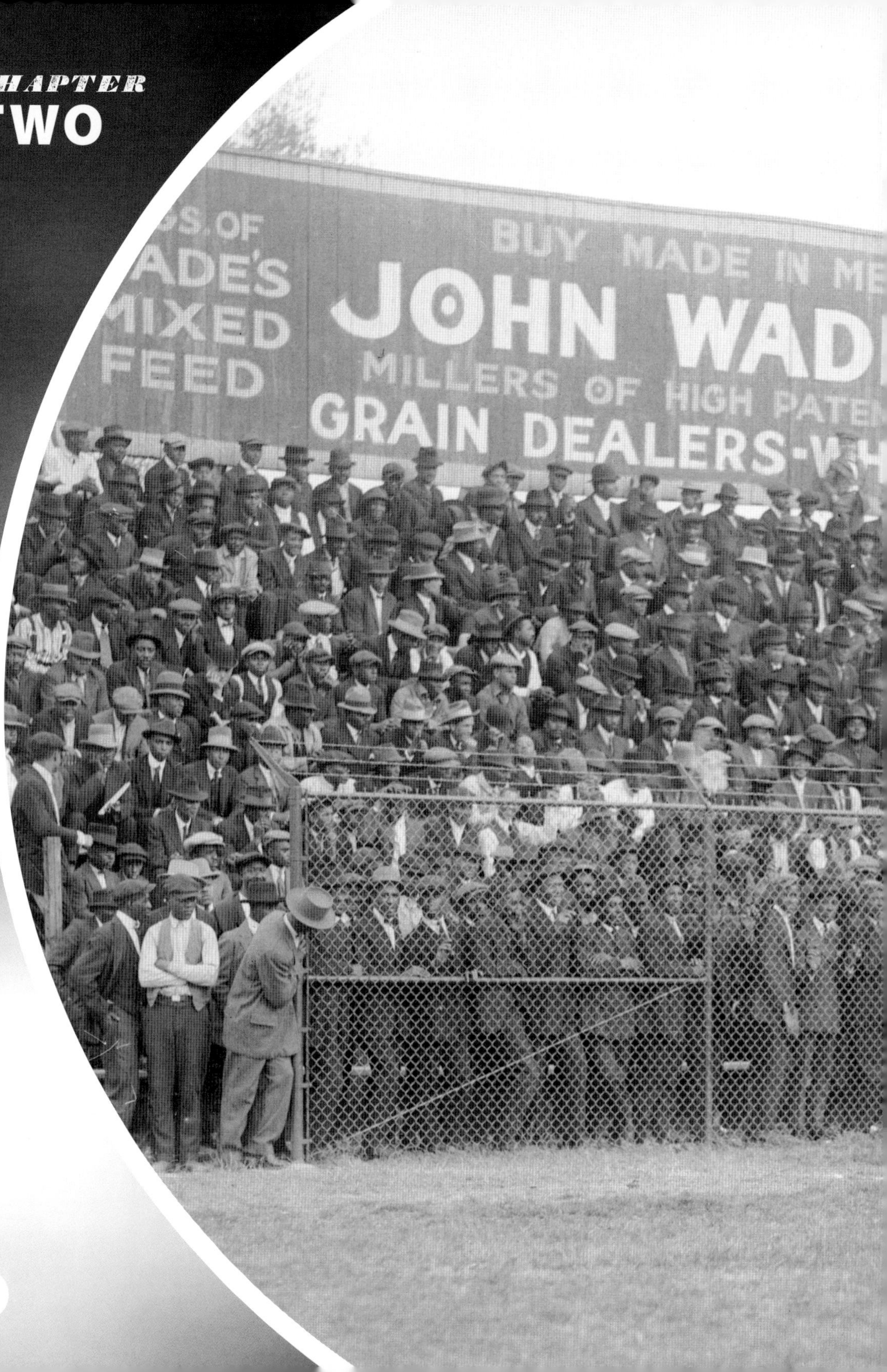
S. OF
ADE'S
MIXED
FEED
BUY MADE IN ME
JOHN WAD
MILLERS OF HIGH PATE
GRAIN DEALERS-W

FORMING THE NEGRO LEAGUES

From the late 1880s to the 1920s, many Black ballplayers joined barnstorming teams. Barnstorming teams traveled and played across the country. They usually played against other barnstorming teams in midwestern towns. Black teams sometimes played against white teams.

Black teams went from town to town looking for anyone who would play them. They sold tickets and split the money with the home team. But the players themselves made

In the early 1900s, Black spectators had to stay in segregated areas at baseball games.

very little. Their schedules were long, and the road trips were tiresome.

The crowds at barnstorming games were separated by ropes. Black fans were on one side of a rope. White fans were on the other. White fans often cheered on the Black players during a game. But after the games, the players faced discrimination wherever they went. They were barred from certain hotels and restaurants because of the color of their skin.

In the early 1900s, Foster, *seated, middle*, owned and managed the professional Black baseball team the Chicago American Giants.

Barnstorming teams sometimes played two or three games a day. They were on the road for most of the year. When there was nowhere to stay, they slept in their buses on the side of the road.

NEW LEAGUES

Andrew "Rube" Foster wanted Black players to have the same opportunities as white players. Foster was an African American baseball player and team manager in the early 1900s. He came up with the idea for an all-Black professional baseball league.

In 1920 Foster organized a meeting of eight officials. The officials were the heads of eight Black barnstorming teams. Foster and these men formed the Negro National League (NNL), an all-Black professional baseball league. The league was based in the Midwest.

The NNL teams continued barnstorming to appeal to their rural fans.

LATINOS IN THE NEGRO LEAGUES

In the late 1800s, baseball was widely popular in Latin America. The first baseball league outside North America was founded in Cuba in 1878. Soon, Latin American countries were developing players who were good enough for the major leagues. The major leagues did not specifically ban Latinos. But Latinos were still not considered equal to white players. Latino players with light skin could pass for white and got a chance to play. Some Latinos of African descent had dark skin. These players were forced to play in the Negro Leagues.

Teams played between 50 and 150 games each year. In 1923 Black teams in the Northeast formed the Eastern Colored League, following the NNL's example.

Negro League players faced discrimination. Teams had trouble booking stadiums. Sometimes hotels would not accommodate them. Foster worked hard to overcome these challenges. The NNL soon became one of the largest Black-owned businesses in the country. But Foster had many doubts and fears. He worried that the NNL would fall apart. He worked long hours. He was hospitalized for exhaustion in the late 1920s. He later died in 1930. Without him, the NNL did fall apart.

EXPLORE ONLINE

Chapter Two discusses how the Negro Leagues were founded. The article at the website below goes into more depth on this topic. How is the information from the website the same as the information in Chapter Two? What new information did you learn?

AFRICAN AMERICAN BASEBALL
abdocorelibrary.com/negro-leagues

CHAPTER
THREE

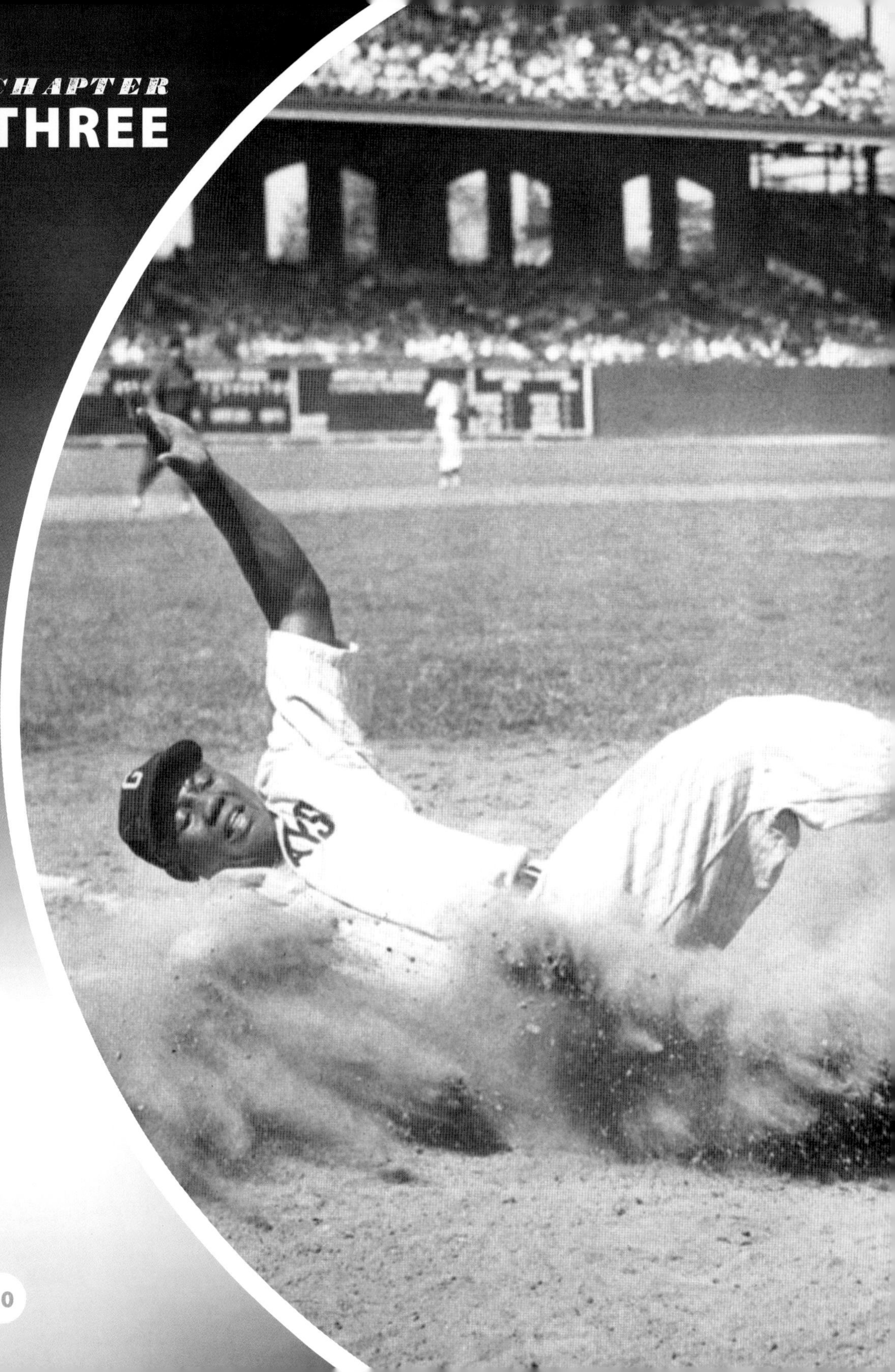

STARTING OVER

After the NNL fell apart in 1931, former NNL teams resumed barnstorming to support themselves. Some teams barnstormed even more after the end of the NNL. The Kansas City Monarchs played up to 250 games a year in the early 1930s.

In 1933 William Augustus "Gus" Greenlee decided to re-form the NNL. Most of the teams in the new NNL league joined from the Eastern Colored League, which had disbanded in 1928.

Greenlee was an African American businessman. He owned his own stadium, so he did not have to pay rent to stadium owners. But he faced other challenges. Many people

Negro League player Josh Gibson slides into home base at the 1944 Negro League All-Star Game.

could not afford to buy tickets to baseball games.

The US economy had collapsed in 1929. Unemployment was high in the 1930s. Many people struggled to make a living. This period was called the Great Depression.

Greenlee came up with new ways for the NNL and its players to make money. He made tickets cheaper. He also started an all-star game. Called the East-West All-Star Game, it was first held in 1933. Much like the MLB All-Star Game that debuted that year, fans were able to see all the

People who were already living in poverty were hit hardest by the Great Depression.

best NNL players in one game. Greenlee asked Black newspapers across the country to publish ballots for the all-star rosters. The ballots allowed readers to vote for the players they wanted to see in the All-Star Game.

In the 1930s, Black newspapers began covering the Negro Leagues. But Negro League news did not reach a wider audience until a New York newspaper called the *Daily Worker* started reporting box scores. The paper's sportswriter, Lester Rodney, organized the first campaign for the end of segregation in baseball. He wrote columns against segregation. He also republished anti-segregation columns from Black papers.

WORLD WAR II

In 1941 the United States entered World War II (1939–1945). Many men left to fight overseas. Some enlisted, or chose to join the US military. Others were drafted, or called up to serve in the military. By late 1942, Black men between the ages of 18 and 37 were included in the draft. They did

TRUJILLO'S TEAM

In 1930 Rafael Trujillo seized control of the Dominican Republic. He was a cruel leader who had his political rivals killed. In 1937 he decided to form a baseball team. He paid Satchel Paige $30,000 to bring the best players from the Negro Leagues to the Dominican Republic. The team was called the Dragones de Ciudad Trujillo. In English, this means the "Dragons of the City Trujillo." The name "Trujillo" was given to the city Santo Domingo. It was named after Rafael Trujillo. The team won a championship in 1937 but did not have as much success as Trujillo wanted. He disbanded the team the next season.

THE NEGRO LEAGUES

NAME	YEAR FORMED	NUMBER OF TEAMS	YEAR DISBANDED
Negro National League	1920	43	1948
Eastern Colored League	1923	11	1928
Negro American League	1937	26	1962

This chart gives information about the three main Negro Leagues. It shows the total number of teams that played in each league during the league's life. Which league had the most teams? How might these numbers reflect the Negro Leagues' popularity in the early 1900s?

not have equal rights. But they were expected to serve their country. More than 100 Negro League players enlisted or were drafted during the war.

Factories and other employers lost workers when men left to fight in the war. There was a high demand for new workers. This opened up opportunities for African American men and women in the workforce. They gained more income from better-paying jobs. More fans could afford tickets to Negro League games.

PLAYING TO STEREOTYPES

People relied on entertainment to raise their spirits during the war. Some teams did their best to entertain fans with more than just baseball. These teams especially tried to appeal to white fans. Syd Pollock, the white owner of the Ethiopian Clowns in Miami, Florida, chose to dress his team in clown outfits. The idea was to make the team more fun and entertaining to white fans. Many people in the Negro Leagues thought this team's owner was making a mockery of the players.

Syd Pollock was also involved with another novelty team, the Zulu Cannibal Giants. The players on this team wore straw dresses and war paint like African tribesmen. In these ways, the team played up racial stereotypes to draw white fans. The team paraded in costumes through towns to draw crowds. Players used fake names that were supposedly African sounding. This meant they could hide the fact that they were playing for the team. Historians have called such teams an embarrassing part of baseball history.

STRAIGHT TO THE
SOURCE

Dave Malarcher was a player in the Negro Leagues. He later became a Negro Leagues manager. He explained how segregation affected Black baseball players:

> I used to have Negroes occasionally tell me, "Do you think Negroes can play in the major leagues?" And do you know what I would say to them? "Do you think so and so here, who is a barber, can cut hair like a white man?" . . . Well, certainly. And I would say, "What's baseball that I can't play it like a white?" . . . The propaganda of keeping the Negro out of the major leagues made even some of the Negroes think that we didn't have the ability.

> Source: John Holway. *Voices from the Great Black Baseball Leagues: Revised Edition.* Mineola, NY: Dover Publications, 2010. Print. 56.

Consider Your Audience

Adapt this passage for a different audience, such as your friends. Write a blog post conveying this information for that audience. How does your post differ from the original text and why?

CHAPTER FOUR

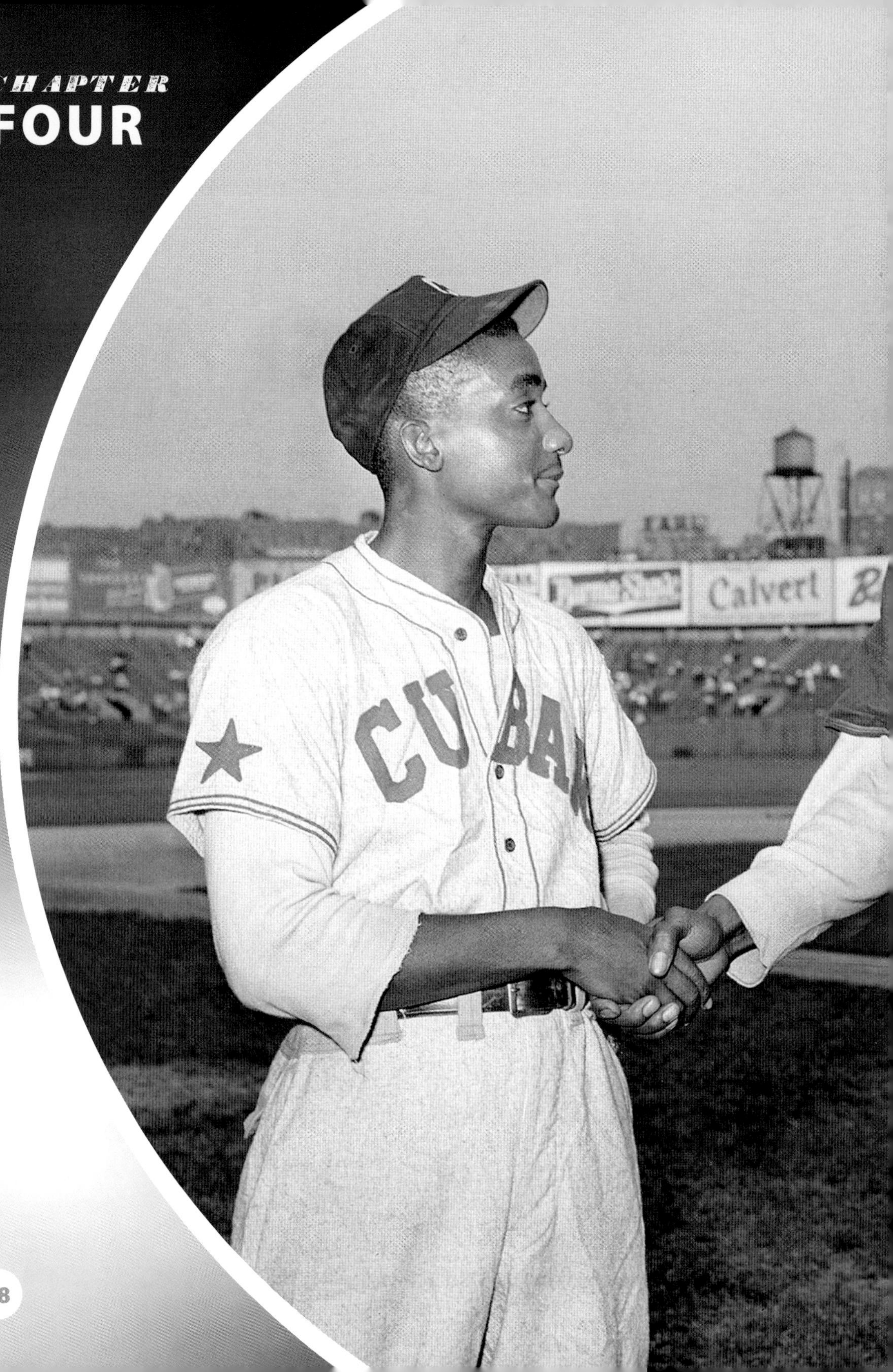

INTEGRATION

Although the Negro Leagues were organized, teams were not very stable. Players often moved from one team to another based on which team could pay more. Teams sometimes canceled league games to play exhibition games that made more money. This instability meant the teams frequently went in and out of business. After World War II ended, the NNL and the Negro American League (NAL) were the

Negro League pitchers David Barnhill, *left*, and Satchel Paige, *right*, shake hands before a game in 1942.

MARSANS AND ALMEIDA

The color barrier restricted opportunities for Black athletes. But some nonwhite athletes were allowed into the major leagues. The first Latino players to play in the major leagues were Rafael Almeida and Armando Marsans. They began playing for the Cincinnati Reds in 1911. They were both of Cuban and Spanish descent. The press focused on their Spanish heritage and their family backgrounds. They were sons of rich landowners. The press thought this would make the players more appealing to fans. Marsans and Almeida were inducted into the Cuban Baseball Hall of Fame in 1939.

only remaining major Negro Leagues. A few minor Negro Leagues continued to survive into the late 1940s and 1950s.

Branch Rickey became the president of the MLB team the Brooklyn Dodgers in the 1940s. He saw how many talented players there were in the Negro Leagues. He knew that getting these players would be a big boost to the Dodgers. He partnered with Gus Greenlee. He told Greenlee that he

Jackie Robinson played for the Kansas City Monarchs for five months before Rickey recruited him.

wanted to form a new Negro League. But that was a lie. Rickey's real plan was to get access to the great Negro League players.

JACKIE ROBINSON

Public support for baseball's integration was growing. Rickey did not want to miss acquiring the best Black players for the Dodgers. In 1945 Rickey identified his first player. It was Negro League infielder Jackie Robinson.

Rickey knew that Black players would likely face abuse from fans and opponents. He wanted a player who would remain calm in these circumstances.

Robinson was a 26-year-old second baseman. He played for the Kansas City Monarchs.

Rickey decided to test Robinson. He took Robinson into a room. He yelled racial insults at Robinson for a long time. But Robinson remained calm. He knew he could not fight back if he wanted to make it in baseball. Rickey knew he'd found the man for the job.

Robinson spent 1946 with the Dodgers' minor league team in Canada. He led the league in batting and stole 40 bases. He showed he was ready to become the first Black baseball player in the major leagues since the late 1800s.

MAKING HISTORY

In January 1947, MLB team owners voted on whether Robinson should be allowed to play. Rickey was the only one who voted in Robinson's favor. Many major league teams threatened to strike if Robinson played. But MLB commissioner Happy Chandler defended Robinson's right to play in the major leagues. He said that Black

Robinson, *right*, poses with his Dodgers teammates before his debut major league game on April 15, 1947.

soldiers had fought and died for their country in World War II. For this reason, he said they had the same right to play as white players did. The strike never took place.

On April 15, 1947, more than 26,000 fans came to Ebbets Field in Brooklyn. It was Opening Day. The Dodgers played the Boston Braves. Among those fans, approximately 14,000 were African American. They witnessed a historic moment when Robinson took the field.

Robinson's breaking of the color barrier was a major step toward racial equality. African American fans all over the country saw that someone like them could play professional sports at the highest level.

JOSH GIBSON

Many people have called Negro Leagues hitter Josh Gibson one of the best ballplayers of all time. Some historians estimate that he hit as many as 900 home runs. He was also a great catcher. Gibson faced many difficulties throughout his life and career. His wife died in childbirth in 1930. After her death, Gibson struggled with substance abuse and mental health issues. He never signed with a major league team. He died at the age of 35. He was inducted into the National Baseball Hall of Fame in 1972.

MOVING TO THE MAJORS

After Robinson's successful debut, other MLB teams began signing Black players to contracts. Negro League star Larry Doby soon followed Robinson into the major leagues. He joined the Cleveland Indians later in the 1947 season. Others followed in 1948. Satchel Paige was one of the best pitchers in the Negro Leagues. For many years, it had been his dream to play in the major leagues. When integration finally happened, Paige was 41 years old. Many people thought he was too old to play in the major leagues. But the Cleveland Indians signed Paige. He became the oldest rookie major league player of all time. He helped the Indians win the World Series in 1948.

As major league teams signed more Black players, the Negro Leagues lost players. The NNL lost money as its star players left. The NNL disbanded in 1948.

Negro League team owners could not compete with the major leagues. Their funding was running low. By 1949 only the NAL remained. All other Negro Leagues had disbanded.

FURTHER EVIDENCE

Chapter Four discusses the breaking of the color barrier. What was one of the main points of this chapter? What evidence is included to support this point? Read the article at the website below. Does the information on the website support this point? Does it present new evidence?

JACKIE ROBINSON BREAKS THE COLOR BARRIER
abdocorelibrary.com/negro-leagues

CHAPTER FIVE

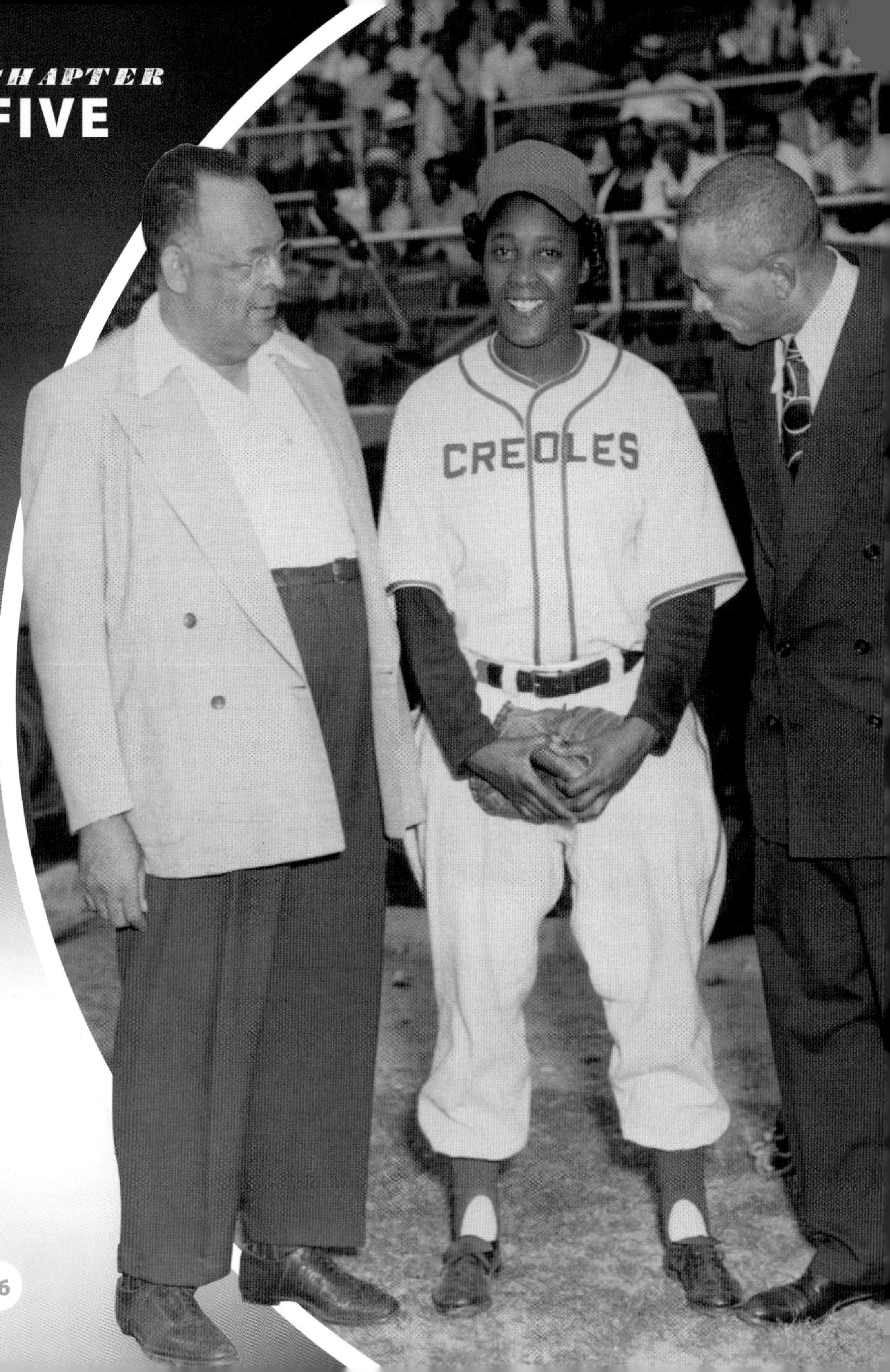

ENDS AND BEGINNINGS

In the 1950s, the NAL had to get creative to compete with the major leagues. Some NAL players had joined the major leagues. NAL games had smaller crowds than MLB games did. The Indianapolis Clowns (formerly the Ethiopian Clowns) were an NAL team. The Clowns signed white players and a female player to attract crowds. The female player was Toni Stone. Stone had played in the minor Negro Leagues. She became the first female regular player on a big-league baseball team in 1953. The Clowns signed her to sell tickets. But Stone took her career seriously. She was an impressive hitter. Still, not everyone was thrilled

Toni Stone was a pioneering baseball player in the 1950s.

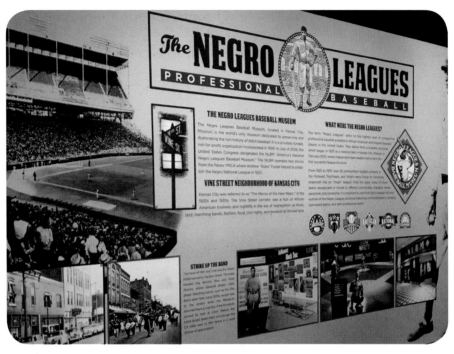

Today, the Negro Leagues Baseball Museum in Kansas City, Missouri, helps preserve the history of the Negro Leagues.

to have her on the team. The Clowns sent her to play for the Kansas City Monarchs in 1954. The Monarchs rarely gave her playing time. Stone left the Monarchs and retired from organized baseball in 1955.

Both the Clowns and the Monarchs competed in barnstorming and regular league games to help attract fans. But by 1962, the NAL had folded. The Clowns continued as an independent team. They played exhibition games until they disbanded in the late 1980s.

THE GAME TODAY

Many former Negro League players went on to have successful careers in the major leagues. Robinson and Doby both became stars. They were inducted into the National Baseball Hall of Fame. Willie Mays, Ernie Banks, and Hank Aaron also played in the Negro Leagues before going on to Hall of Fame careers. Mays was an excellent hitter and outfielder for the New York Giants and San Francisco Giants. Banks spent 19 years with the Chicago Cubs. He is considered

SATCHEL PAIGE

Pitcher Satchel Paige was popular among both Black and white fans. His career was defined by showmanship. One of Paige's showstopping tricks was to call in all his outfielders to sit down next to him by the pitcher's mound. He was so confident he would strike out the batter that he thought they would not be needed in the field. Because of the color barrier, Paige did not make his MLB debut until 1948. Paige never truly retired, even getting one more MLB start at the age of 59 with the Oakland Athletics. He was elected to the National Baseball Hall of Fame in 1971.

THE NEGRO LEAGUES BASEBALL MUSEUM

In 1991 the Negro Leagues Baseball Museum opened in Kansas City, Missouri. This museum shares the history of the Negro Leagues and their legacy. It showcases historic artifacts such as players' jerseys. Raymond Doswell selects the artifacts for the museum. He said, "At the museum we're trying to tell the cultural history with the context of segregation. . . . Baseball is a great on-ramp to discussing race and societal issues. It isn't played in a vacuum."

one of the greatest infielders of all time. Aaron broke Babe Ruth's MLB home run record of 714 while playing for the Atlanta Braves in 1974. He retired two years later with 755 home runs.

Black players integrated MLB in the mid-1900s. By 1981 a record 18.7 percent of MLB players were African American. But by 2018, that number had fallen to 8.4 percent. Cost is one major factor. Approximately 45 percent of African American children live below the poverty line. Baseball requires equipment, including

BLACK BALLPLAYERS

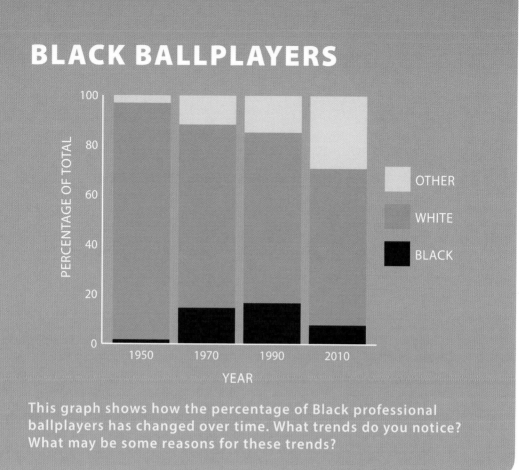

This graph shows how the percentage of Black professional ballplayers has changed over time. What trends do you notice? What may be some reasons for these trends?

a ball, bat, and glove. Sports such as basketball and soccer only require a ball.

In 1989 MLB started a program to help people of color get involved in baseball. The program is called Reviving Baseball in Inner Cities (RBI). RBI provides opportunities for inner-city youth to play baseball. Programs such as RBI help ensure the legacy of integrated baseball continues with equal opportunities.

FAST FACTS

- In 1887 the International League, a minor baseball league, forbade its teams from signing Black players.

- In the late 1800s and early 1900s, many Black ballplayers joined barnstorming teams. They traveled and played against local teams. They faced discrimination and segregation.

- Andrew "Rube" Foster formed the first all-Black professional baseball league, the Negro National League (NNL), in 1920.

- Foster died in 1930. The NNL folded one year later.

- Black businessman William Augustus "Gus" Greenlee re-formed the NNL in 1933.

- Some Negro Leagues folded after World War II ended in 1945. The NNL and the Negro American League (NAL) were the only remaining major Negro Leagues.

- Black ballplayer Jackie Robinson debuted with the Brooklyn Dodgers on April 15, 1947. He helped break the color barrier. Other major league teams later signed Black players. As a result, the Negro Leagues lost players and money. The NNL disbanded in 1948. The NAL folded in 1962.

- Today, Major League Baseball helps get people of color involved in baseball through its Reviving Baseball in Inner Cities program.

STOP AND
THINK

Surprise Me

Chapter Two describes how the Negro Leagues were formed. After reading this book, what two or three facts about the early years of the Negro Leagues surprised you the most? Write one or two sentences about each fact. Why did you find each fact surprising?

Why Do I Care?

Even though the Jim Crow era is over and the color barrier is broken, there are still inequalities in baseball. Why do you think this is? How do you think racial inequalities in sports affect other aspects of people's lives?

You Are There

This book discusses the Negro Leagues. Imagine you were a baseball fan attending a Negro League game in the 1940s. Write a letter home telling your friends about the experience. What do you notice about the game? Be sure to add plenty of details to your letter.

GLOSSARY

barnstorming
in sports, touring and playing informal games with local teams

discrimination
the unjust treatment of a group of people based on their race, gender, or other characteristics

economy
a system in which goods and services are exchanged

exhibition game
an unofficial, off-season game played by professional teams

prejudice
a feeling of dislike toward a group of people based on their race or other characteristics

propaganda
untrue or exaggerated ideas that are spread to influence people

roster
an official list of people who are on a team

rural
located in the country

segregation
the separation of people based on race or other factors

stereotype
a common belief about a group of people that is usually negative and untrue

ONLINE
RESOURCES

To learn more about the Negro Leagues, visit our free resource websites below.

Visit **abdocorelibrary.com** or scan this QR code for free Common Core resources for teachers and students, including vetted activities, multimedia, and booklinks, for deeper subject comprehension.

Visit **abdobooklinks.com** or scan this QR code for free additional online weblinks for further learning. These links are routinely monitored and updated to provide the most current information available.

LEARN
MORE

DeMocker, Michael. *Barnstorming*. Kennett Square, PA: Purple Toad Publishing, 2017.

Harris, Duchess, and Tom Streissguth. *Jackie Robinson Breaks Barriers*. Minneapolis, MN: Abdo Publishing, 2019.

ABOUT THE
AUTHORS

Duchess Harris, JD, PhD

Dr. Harris is a professor of American Studies at Macalester College and curator of the Duchess Harris Collection of ABDO books. She is also the coauthor of the titles in the collection, which features popular selections such as *Hidden Human Computers: The Black Women of NASA* and series including News Literacy and Being Female in America.

Before working with ABDO, Dr. Harris authored several other books on the topics of race, culture, and American history. She served as an associate editor for *Litigation News*, the American Bar Association Section of Litigation's quarterly flagship publication, and was the first editor in chief of *Law Raza*, an interactive online journal covering race and the law, published at William Mitchell College of Law. She has earned a PhD in American Studies from the University of Minnesota and a JD from William Mitchell College of Law.

Alex Kies

Alex Kies lives in Saint Paul, Minnesota, with a cat named Hippolyta. Besides baseball, he's written about professional wrestling, teleportation, literature, and politics. He's left-handed.

INDEX